## DIGGING UP THE PAST

# MACHU PICCHU
## CITY IN THE CLOUDS

Barbara A. Somervill

**HIGH**
interest
**books**

Children's Press
A Division of Scholastic Inc.
New York / Toronto / London / Auckland / Sydney
Mexico City / New Delhi / Hong Kong
Danbury, Connecticut

Book Design: Jennifer Crilly
Contributing Editors: Matthew Pitt and Geeta Sobha
Photo Credits: Cover, p. 1 © Darrell Gulin/Corbis; p. 4 © Mark A. Johnson/Corbis; p. 7
© Jeremy Horner/Corbis; p. 8 © 2002 Geoatlas; p. 11 © Christie's Images/Corbis; p. 13
© Charles & Josette Lenars/Corbis; p. 15 © Corbis; p. 16 © Hulton-Deutsch/Corbis;
pp. 19, 27, 36, 39 © Reuters/Corbis; p. 20 © Dave G. Houser/Corbis; p. 23
© Bettmann/Corbis; p. 25 © Werner Forman/Corbis; p. 28 © John Van Hasselt/Corbis
Sygma; pp. 31, 35, 41 © Wolfgang Kaehler/Corbis; p. 33 © Chris Rainier/Corbis

Library of Congress Cataloging-in-Publication Data

Somervill, Barbara A.
    Machu Picchu : city in the clouds / Barbara A. Somervill.
    p. cm. — (Digging up the past)
    Includes bibliographical references and index.
    ISBN 0-516-25123-6 (lib. bdg.) — ISBN 0-516-25092-2 (pbk.)
    1. Incas—History—Juvenile literature. 2. Incas—Antiquities—Juvenile
    literature. 3. Machu Picchu Site (Peru)—Juvenile literature. 4. Cuzco
    Region (Peru) Antiquities—Juvenile literature. I. Title. II. Digging up the past
    (Children's Press)

    F3429.1.M3S65 2005
    985'.37019—dc22

                                            2004023907

1 2 3 4 5 6 7 8 9 10 R 14 13 12 11 10 09 08 07 06 05

# CONTENTS

The ancient Inca city of Machu Picchu is located at 7,710 feet (2,350 meters) above sea level. At this great height, the peak of the mountain is often surrounded by clouds. That is the reason why Machu Picchu is nicknamed "City in the Clouds."

# Introduction

A group of hikers board a train in Cuzco, Peru, in South America. They store their backpacks and settle down for the ride. As the train picks up speed, the fast-flowing Urubamba River can be seen from the windows. The train snakes its way through the river valley. It is headed for the city in the clouds.

Four hours later, the train grinds to a halt. The hikers find an ancient trail once used by the Inca people. The hikers climb high into the Andes Mountains. The air is thin. They begin to get dizzy. Some get headaches or feel sick to their stomachs.

The group camps for the night. The hikers eat a meal of rice and corn, followed by a sweet purple corn dessert called *mazamorra morada* (**maz**-a-mor-ra **mo**-ra-da).

In the morning, the hikers awaken to a cold mist that covers the peaks of the Andes Mountains. The group begins to climb higher on the trail. As they walk, the cold mist is burned away by strong sunlight.

Suddenly, the mountain peak Huayna Picchu (**whan**-ah **pee**-chu) comes into view. The hikers gasp. They are looking at the ruins of the ancient mountain city of Machu Picchu (**mah**-chu **pee**-chu).

Some of the hikers in the group thought they would never get the chance to visit this magnificent site. But here is the ancient city, sitting on top of a mountain surrounded by clouds!

Archaeologists and tourists visit Machu Picchu regularly to learn about Incan life. Scientists have have been studying the city for almost one hundred years to uncover all of its secrets. What makes this ancient site such a wonder to people all over the world? Let's find out.

The steps shown here are an old Inca trail leading to Machu Picchu.

Ecuador

Colombia

*Amazon River*

Peru

Brazil

● Lima

*Urubamba River*

● Machu Picchu

Bolivia

*Pacific Ocean*

*Lake Titicaca*

Incan Territory

Chile

The Inca built a grand empire that grew to cover 350,000 square miles (906 square kilometers). It covered present-day Peru and parts of present-day Ecuador, Bolivia, Chile, and Argentina.

# CHAPTER ONE

# Understanding the Incas

The Incan civilization began in about A.D. 1200. Its founder was a man named Manco Capac. Manco Capac built the village of Cuzco in a valley of the Andes Mountains in present-day Peru. The Inca people were ruled by an emperor. The emperor and his relatives were considered true Incas. They made up the ruling government.

The Inca empire grew slowly. Great changes did not come until the fifteenth century when the ninth emperor, Pachacuti, began his rule. Pachacuti led the growth of Incan civilization. During Pachacuti's rule, the empire stretched 3,400 miles (5,500 kilometers). People from areas of present-day Ecuador and Chile were conquered. These people became part of the Inca empire.

## Pachacuti's Legend

Pachacuti was not supposed to be the emperor. The story of how he came to be ruler is a popular Andes legend. In 1438, Pachacuti's father, Viracocha, was the Incan ruler. By tradition, the ruler's first son was to become the next emperor. This was Pachacuti's older brother. That year, the Inca people were fighting a fierce rival, the Chanca tribe. The Chanca planned to attack Cuzco.

Viracocha and his oldest son feared the Chanca. Terrified, they fled into the mountains to hide from the threat. According to legend, Pachacuti decided to face the threat. He gathered warriors, and they dressed in jaguar skins. The Incas admired jaguars for their cunning and power.

Pachacuti was leading a very small army against the Chanca warriors. Incan legends say that their Sun god, Inti, aided Pachacuti. Inti turned the stones on the battlefield into Incan warriors. These stone warriors helped Pachacuti destroy the Chanca army and save Cuzco.

Pachacuti was now emperor. He quickly conquered other cultures and built new cities. During Pachacuti's rule, no one went hungry or homeless. There was very little crime. That's probably because the punishment for most crimes was death!

This painting shows many emperors of the Inca empire. The Inca believed that the emperors were related to the Sun god, Inti. The emperors had complete control over the empire.

## Inca Life

The people of the Inca empire completed many projects. They built outstanding irrigation systems, which helped carry water into villages and homes. They also built palaces, temples, and roadways. Building these structures could be backbreaking work. Incas did not know about wheels. They did not use large animals to carry heavy items. Yet the workers built 15,000 miles (24,000 km) of paved roads. They erected buildings, using stones weighing many tons. Much of this work was performed 3 miles (4.8 km) above sea level, where the air was thin and there is less oxygen. Thin air causes some people to get sick or be unable to function properly. Many people today are amazed that the Incas worked so hard at this height.

The Inca masons who carved stones for buildings were incredibly skilled. Each stone fit the one beside it perfectly, like pieces of a jigsaw puzzle. Even now, five hundred years later, a knife blade cannot be slipped between the stones.

The Incas did not have a written language. How did they keep track of important information without written words? The Incas recorded information on a tool called a *quipu* (**kee**-pu). The *quipu* used a system of knots that were tied into a string. Each knot kept track of different information such as the number of babies born or the amount of crops being grown.

## Labor Tax

The Incas did not use money. Most people were farmers who supported their families and the emperor with their produce. Families kept one-third of their crops or goods for their own survival.

Another third went to the government as tax. The government stored those food supplies in case of poor crop harvests. The last third of the crops were used in temples, for sacrifices and religious feasts.

Incan men also paid tax with physical labor. In Incan culture, men were required to work for the

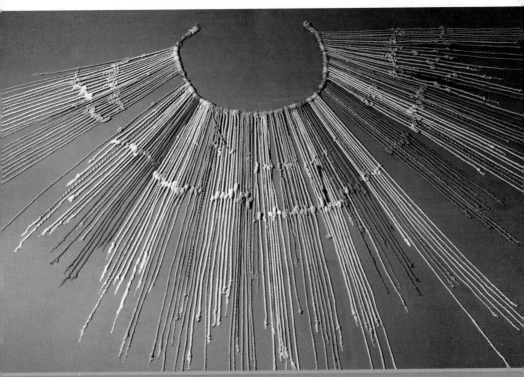

In addition to recording practical information, *quipus* were also used to record historical information. Only specially trained people were able to read *quipus*. The *quipu* shown here is displayed in a museum in Peru.

government for at least two weeks each year. This labor tax was called *mit'a* (**mih**-ta). These workers built temples, palaces, and bridges. They dug canals and irrigation ditches. They maintained the empire's gold and silver mines.

**ARTIFACT**

To the subjects of the Incan empire, gold was forbidden. The Inca believed that gold was the "sweat of the Sun" and belonged to the gods. The emperor was considered the "son of the Sun," so only he and other nobles were allowed to wear gold.

## The Spanish Arrive

By the 1520s, rumors of Incan gold attracted attention from European nations. Gold was far more valuable to Europeans than to the Incas. Spanish explorers and soldiers called conquistadors sailed to the lands of the Incas in search of the precious metal.

The Spaniards' leader was Francisco Pizarro. Although Pizarro led only a small troop of conquistadors, his men conquered the Incan empire. This is partly because the Incan empire

When the Incas first met Francisco Pizarro, they thought that he was their god Viracocha.

was already suffering. The Incas were fighting a terrible disease. The emperor Huayna Capac died of smallpox in 1525. His death left the Incan empire without a ruler. Two of the emperor's sons Huáscar and Atahualpa tried to claim their father's title. A civil war broke out as they fought

Atahualpa became the thirteenth emperor of the Incas after defeating his brother at war. After he won, Atahualpa had his brother put to death.

for control of the empire. Atahualpa was the victor. However, he had killed many Incan nobles during the war. Because of this, the Incan army had few leaders left.

Pizarro saw that the Incan army only took orders from Atahualpa. He captured Atahualpa, leaving the Incan army powerless. To get their leader back, the Incan people paid a huge ransom. It included 13,420 pounds (6,100 kilograms) of gold and 26,000 pounds (11,793 kg) of silver.

## ARTIFACT

The gold and silver given to Pizarro were in the form of items such as plates, jewelry, and statues. Today, that ransom would be worth billions of dollars.

## Broken Promise

Atahualpa should have been released once the ransom was paid. Pizarro, however, would not risk freeing the Incan leader. He had only a few Spanish soldiers. The Incan army, though, had thousands of men. So, instead of keeping his word, Pizarro kept Atahualpa prisoner. Pizarro accused the Inca of serious crimes. In 1533, the Spanish court executed Atahualpa. Soon after Atahualpa's death, the Incan empire died too.

Spanish conquerors demanded that the Incas follow their religion. They believed that everyone should be Catholic. To force the Incas to follow the Catholic religion, the Spanish destroyed Inca temples and holy places. They did many things to harm, and even wipe out, parts of the Inca civilization.

Inca citizens did not give up all of their culture so easily though. They managed to keep some secrets from the Spanish. Centuries later, people would take a new interest in Incan culture. Archaeologists would try to unlock the mysteries of Inca culture.

## VALUE OF CLOTH

Incan women spun and wove cotton and wool to make cloth. Cloth took long hours to produce. The Incas valued cloth more than gold. In fact, the Incas began using cloth like money. They traded cloth for goods at local markets.

Many people of Incan descent honor their past by practicing ceremonies of their ancestors. This priest is taking part in a ceremony to thank mountain spirits.

These steps are actually small farming fields on the slopes of Machu Picchu. They were created by the ancient Incas.

# CHAPTER TWO

# Mysteries Uncovered

## Hiram Bingham

In 1911 Hiram Bingham, a Yale University professor, took a trip to Peru. Bingham had traveled to South America to search for Incan ruins. Bingham trekked to the Urubamba Valley. There, he met with Melchor Arteaga, who lived in the area. Arteaga told Bingham of a city in ruins in the jungle. He informed Bingham that the town was called Machu Picchu, or "Old Mountain." Arteaga agreed to take Bingham there the following day.

The weather was raw and wet the next morning. Bingham's guide knew this bad weather would make the journey a tough one. Arteaga wanted to hold off on traveling. However, Bingham could not wait. He bribed Arteaga with three times his normal daily pay—about fifty cents.

The two men began their long hike. They crossed swollen, rushing rivers on rickety bridges. Bingham crawled across the bridges on his hands and knees.

To clear a path through the jungle growth, they used swords called machetes. Finally, they reached a small farm high in the Andes. There, they rested and ate with the family. After lunch, the farmer's son, Pablito Alvarez, led Bingham to the ruined city.

Bingham's first sight of Machu Picchu shocked him. He could see ancient paved roads and granite palaces. Running water trickled into the old stone fountains and pools. Bingham could not believe how well these ruins were being maintained by the local residents. In fact, the locals were still using the same farming terraces that had been made by the Incas centuries ago. They were growing corn, potatoes, and a grain called quinoa.

## ARTIFACT

Newspapers reported that Bingham "discovered" Machu Picchu. However, local Peruvians knew where it was all along!

## Uncovering the Secrets

Bingham left Peru for a short time, but he soon returned with teams of archaeologists. These people hoped to unlock Machu Picchu's ancient secrets.

Hiram Bingham went on to become governor of Connecticut and a United States senator.

Bingham's crew cleared away vines and grasses. To their amazement, most buildings remained in very good condition. Only the twig and grass roofs of the buildings had decayed.

The crew mapped the locations of the buildings. They identified a central plaza with fountains and pools. They also discovered three temples with huge stone altars. The most important of these buildings was called the Temple of the Sun. It had a curved stone wall. During certain days of the year, shadows fell on a sacred object inside the temple. The Incas believed the Sun to be godlike. Where the Sun rose and fell was of great importance. It had great religious value to the Incas. Studying the Sun's path was practical too. It helped inform Incas when to plant their crops.

## Amazing Artifacts

Bingham's crew found hundreds of small artifacts. They dug up jars and mugs. They found ceramic bottles called *aryballos* (ahr-**ee**-bahl-los). Larger vats that had been used to store grain were uncovered. The team also recovered many plates. These plates were often decorated with animals, such as pumas and condors. Bingham's crew was overjoyed that these items had survived the centuries.

Diggers also found many metal items such as bronze axes and chisels at Machu Picchu. These tools were probably used in Machu Picchu's construction.

Incan gold figures like this statue were found at Machu Picchu. Gold and silver objects of the Incas are rare. The Spanish melted most of these objects and sent the gold to Spain.

Archaeologists also found Incan jewelry worn by both male and female nobles. Women used shawl pins to fasten their cloaks together. Gold or silver ear spools marked a man as an adult noble. These ear spools were like giant earrings, and were often three inches (7.5 centimeters) wide. Male Inca nobles would stretch their earlobes and cut the skin. Then they would fit the ear spools inside. Needless to say, this was a painful piercing!

## Afterlife in the Andes

One of the most exciting discoveries was the one hundred and thirty-five skeletons found near Machu Picchu. Scientists in the crew studied the bones carefully. They guessed that the skeletons had come from one hundred and nine adult females, twenty-two adult males, and four children. The Incas buried corpses with items that the dead would need in the next life. This included items such as dried corn or statues of birds and llamas. Those burying a corpse then used yards of cloth to wrap the body.

Today, archaeologists continue to uncover remains of the Incas. In 1999, sixteen tombs were discovered at Sacsayhuaman in Cuzco.

Many Incan mummies were found buried along with everyday items, such as food, utensils, and even valuables. The Inca worshipped their ancestors and provided these items as gifts to the dead.

# CHAPTER THREE

# Changing Views

Hiram Bingham and his team continued to find Incan artifacts. The more they discovered, the more they learned about Incan culture. Bingham's crew found knives that priests used to kill animals as religious sacrifices. Most of these religious sacrifices were of animals like guinea pigs or llamas.

Occasionally, the Incas sacrificed humans. The earliest reports of Incan human sacrifice came from the Spanish conquerors who witnessed them taking place. After many years of study, archaeologists now believe that once a year, each region sent two children to the Inca capital, Cuzco. The children, called *capacochas* (cah-pah-**koh**-kas), were honored, attended feasts, and went home. There, local priests clubbed them to death as a sacrifice to the Sun god. But their execution was not a punishment. The Incas considered being chosen for a sacrifice a high honor.

Bingham and his crew spent long months studying their incredible find. They began focusing more energy on Machu Picchu's many temples. They continued finding sacred artifacts. This made Bingham believe that Machu Picchu had been a religious center. He thought that the female skeletons belonged to *acllas* (**ahk**-yes). *Acllas* were Incan holy women. Bingham's group knew that *acllas* were sacrificed after earthquakes and droughts. They guessed that these women had been sacrificed after natural disasters.

## New Clues, New Tools

Machu Picchu thrilled Hiram Bingham and his crew. They longed to know who used it, and for what

### WHICH CITY DID HE FIND?

When Bingham first began his archaeological dig, he did not know that it was Machu Picchu he was exploring! There was another important Incan city called Vilcabamba. This was believed to be the last Incan capital. Bingham guessed that he had rediscovered Vilcabamba, not Machu Picchu.

This building is the Temple of the Sun, which is also called the Sacred Rock, at Machu Picchu.

purposes. However, the technology that Bingham used to help his search is now outdated. Today, archaeologists use more sophisticated tools in their searches. This helps them better understand and study artifacts. Computers and scientific instruments test artifacts. They can determine which materials were used to make artifacts. They can also determine when the artifact was made.

Many modern archaeologists continue to be fascinated by Machu Picchu. These scientists include Richard Burger and Lucy Salazar of Yale University. The two have carefully studied this city in the clouds. They have made new guesses. For instance, very few weapons were found at Machu Picchu. This led Burger and Salazar to believe the city was never a fortress. Instead, it was probably a kind of ancient resort. They believe Machu Picchu served as a vacation home for the emperor and his extended family. As Bingham believed, Machu Picchu may have also been a religious center.

Archaeologists have used new instruments to test the bones Bingham found. The instruments revealed that the bones came from an equal number of male and female skeletons. This is different from what Bingham's crew believed. Also, most of Machu Picchu's corpses were not the result of human sacrifice. These people died of natural causes.

These are important discoveries. Archaeologists hope to learn more in the future. The Incas had no written history. They did not leave behind records of how they lived. Because of this, many of Machu Picchu's mysteries remain out of reach.

Throughout the Incan empire were water systems, such as aqueducts and sewers. Most were destroyed by the Spanish invaders. This sewer is located at Machu Picchu and is one of the few remaining.

## Building on the Mountain

Modern engineers have focused on Machu Picchu's magnificent architecture. Many of the stones used to build Machu Picchu weigh over a ton (0.9 metric ton). Moving them must have been difficult without help from wheels or large animals.

One modern engineer, Ken Wright, studied the Incan water system. Wright found that Machu Picchu's water system was still working in the 1990s.

He learned that the Incas built holding ponds. These helped catch fresh springwater. Underground pipes transported running water to fountains and baths. A sewer system removed wastewater.

## Looking to the Skies

These days, those interested in Machu Picchu are studying the sky. Astronomy was an important part of Incan culture. Incas carefully tracked the Sun, Moon, and stars. Their measurements were very accurate. These heavenly bodies were an important part of Incan religion.

One object found at Machu Picchu was a large stone altar. This object is known as the *intihuatana* (in-tih-**wah**-tan-ah). Astronomy experts studied this Machu Picchu altar carefully. They witnessed dark shadows falling on the *intihuatana* at noon each day. However, there are two exceptions. At noon on March 21 and September 21, the Sun casts no shadows on the altar. These two dates mark the start of spring and autumn. Based on this fact, experts believe that the altar was probably used to determine the changing of a year's seasons.

*Intihuatana* means for tying the Sun. Inca priests held ceremonies to keep sunlight longer during the winter days.

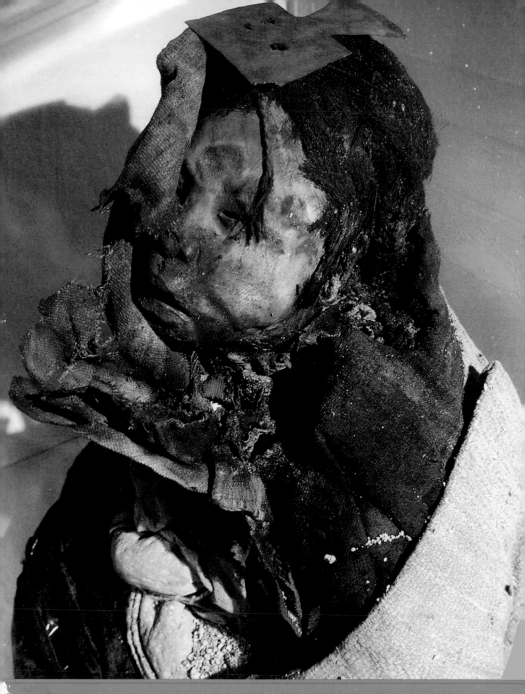

This mummy of a young girl was found on Mount Llulliallaco in Argentina by Johan Reinhard. Mount Llulliallaco is the highest archaeological site in the world.

# CHAPTER FOUR

# A Lasting Heritage

The Incan civilization has been gone for centuries. Hiram Bingham is no longer alive. However, Bingham's curiosity lives on in other people. Today's archaeologists continue to study Machu Picchu. They have explored other sites too. Discoveries about Peru's rich past are still being made today.

## Mountain Mummies

In 1995, an American named Johan Reinhard made a startling discovery. He was exploring the slopes of Mount Ampato in the Andes. There, 20,000 feet (6,096 m) above sea level, Reinhard stumbled upon a frozen corpse. The body belonged to an adolescent girl. The girl, later named Juanita, had lived in Incan times. Mountain ice had preserved her body for more than five hundred years. With further study, her bones, muscles, and organs may reveal many mysteries. They could provide scientists with knowledge about Incan health and eating habits.

Better-preserved bodies have also been found. In 2000, scientists discovered thousands of Incan mummies under Tupac Amaru. Tupac Amaru is a town near Lima, Peru's capital. Many mummies still had visible facial expressions. Scientists were able to study their hair, skin, and eyes.

## ARTIFACT

Often, several family members were wrapped in one mummy bundle.

## The Latest Searches

In recent years, explorers have found two other lost Incan cities near Machu Picchu. The second city, Llactapata, was discovered in November 2003. Because of the dense jungle, finding Llactapata was not easy. However, new technology helped the search. Explorers used photographs that were taken from the sky. These photographs helped the explorers locate Llactapata, even through the thick jungle. The team then relied on older tools, hacking through the jungle with machetes to reach their discovery.

On July 28, 2001, Alejandro Toledo was the first Quechua person to be elected president of Peru.

## Protecting Machu Picchu

In recent years, Machu Picchu has become a major tourist destination. A group called UNESCO named it a World Heritage site. UNESCO stands for the United Nations Educational, Scientific and Cultural Organization. UNESCO deeply values Machu Picchu. They know the site can teach us much about Inca culture. The site's architecture and artifacts help tourists understand the Inca people.

More than 300,000 people visit the site each year. They admire the skill of Incan builders. They take photos and dream of ancient days. They are there to soak up Machu Picchu's rich history. However, they may be placing Machu Picchu at risk.

Some scientists fear that tourism could eventually damage or destroy Machu Picchu. They warn that so much human traffic might cause a landslide. Machu Picchu's buildings could fall into the Urubamba River, hundreds of feet below. The ancient site would then be lost forever.

In 1999, UNESCO threatened to take away Machu Picchu's World Heritage listing. That's because some people in Peru were planning to build a cable car system. UNESCO was concerned that the system would only increase the number of tourists. This could increase the risk to this valuable Inca site.

Peru's president Alejandro Toledo agreed. He decided to stop plans to expand Machu Picchu tourism. For now, the cable car system is on hold. Tourists can still visit. They simply have to trek the Incan trail. Those who reach this majestic site know the journey is worth it. Once they get to Machu Picchu, their imaginations may wander and run wild. It is easy to get excited while thinking about the Incan empire's many mysteries.

Today, tourists from all over the world visit Machu Picchu to get a glimpse of the world of the ancient Incas.

# New Words

*acllas* (**ahk**-yes) Incan holy women

**archaeologist** (ar-kee-**ol**-o-gist) someone who studies the past by digging up old buildings and objects and examining them carefully

**architecture** (**ar**-ki-tek-chur) the science or art of building design

**artifacts** (**art**-uh-fakts) objects made by people who lived long ago

*aryballos* (ahr-**ee**-bahl-los) ceramic bottles

*capacochas* (ca-pah-**koh**-kas) children in ancient Incan times who were chosen, honored, and then sacrificed to the Sapa Inca

**conquistadors** (con-**keys**-ta-dors) leaders in the Spanish conquest of the Americas

**dense** (**denss**) crowded or thick

*intihuatana* (in-tih-**wah**-tan-ah) a large stone altar found at Machu Picchu

**irrigation** (**ihr**-uh-ga-shun) a system of supplying water using artificial means

**machete** (muh-**shet**-ee) a long, heavy knife with a broad blade

# New Words

**mason** (**may**-suhn) someone who builds or works with stone, cement, or bricks

**mazamorra morada** (maz-a-**mor**-ra **mo**-ra-da) a sweet purple corn dessert

**mit'a** (**mih**-ta) a tax on labor in Inca culture in which men had to work for the government two weeks out of every year

**quinoa** (**keen**-wa) a weed of the Andes whose seeds are ground and used as food

**quipu** (**kee**-pu) a string of knots on which the Incas recorded all their information since they did not have a written language; for example, a red knot might mean a new baby

**ransom** (**ran**-suhm) money that is demanded before someone who is being held captive can be set free

**rickety** (**rik**-uh-tee) old, weak, and likely to break

**smallpox** (**smawl**-poks) a very contagious disease that causes chills, high fever, and pimples that can leave permanent scars

**sophisticated** (suh-**fiss**-tuh-kay-tid) cleverly designed and able to do difficult or complicated things

# For Further Reading

Bernand, Carmen. *Incas: People of the Sun.* New York: Harry N. Abrams, Incorporated, 1994.

Lewin, Ted. *Lost City: The Discovery of Machu Picchu.* New York: Philomel Books, 2003.

Lourie, Peter. *Lost Treasure of the Inca.* Honesdale, PA: Boyds Mills Press, 2003.

Mann, Elizabeth. *Machu Picchu: The Story of the Amazing Incas and Their City in the Clouds.* New York: Mikaya Press, 2003.

Reinhard, Johan. *Discovering the Inca Ice Maiden: My Adventures on Ampato.* Washington, D.C.: National Geographic Society, 1998.

Sayer, Chloe. *The Incas.* Austin, TX: Steck-Vaughn Company, 1999.

# Resources

## Organizations

**Instituto Machu Picchu**
San Fernando 287, Miraflores
Lima 18, Peru
*e-mail: machupicchu@imapi.org.pe*

**World Heritage Centre**
**UNESCO**
7, place de Fontenoy
75352 Paris 07SP
France
*e-mail: wh-info@unesco.org*

## Web Sites

**Machu Picchu and the Inca Way of Life**
*www.shastahome.com/machu-picchu/guide.html*
This site offers information on Inca culture,
religion, and daily life.

# Resources

### The Machu Picchu Library
*www.machupicchu.org/library*
This site provides links to various Web sites about Machu Picchu and Inca history.

### National Geographic: Inca Mummies
*www.nationalgeographic.com/inca*
Enjoy an archaeological dig when you log on to this site.

### Nova Online Adventure: The Lost Empire
*www.pbs.org/wgbh/nova/peru/worlds*
Explore the world of the ancient Incas by logging on to this Web site.

# Index

# Index

## About the Author

Barbara A. Somervill writes books for children, as well as articles and textbooks. Barbara was raised and educated in New York. She has also lived in Canada, Australia, California, and South Carolina. She is an avid reader and enjoys movies and live theater.